DATE DUE

MAY 19 2002	

GERMANY SURRENDERS

1 9 4 5

Introduction by James J. Hastings and Goddard Winterbottom

National Archives and Records Administration, Washington, DC

Published for the
National Archives and Records Administration
By the National Archives Trust Fund Board
1989

Library of Congress Cataloging-in-Publication Data

Germany surrenders, 1945.

  (Milestone documents in the National Archives)
  Rev. ed. of: World War II surrender documents. Germany surrenders, 1945. 1976.
  Bibliography: p.
  1. World War, 1939-1945—Peace—Sources. 2. World War, 1939-1945—Germany—Sources. 3. Germany—History—1933-1945—Sources. I. United States. National Archives and Records Administration. II. World War II surrender documents. Germany surrenders, 1945. III. Series.
D814.1.G47 1989   940.53′14   88-33033
ISBN 0-911333-17-7

AN INTRODUCTION

World War II, the deadliest war in history, began in Europe with the German invasion of Poland, September 1, 1939. For almost 6 years it raged across the Western World, taking the lives of 11 million soldiers and an equal number of civilians. Finally, by the spring of 1945, the major Allies—the United States, the Soviet Union, Great Britain, and France—had brought to exhaustion the will and fighting capacity of the German war machine. Slowly but completely, the Nazi-led Third Reich collapsed, not in a single surrender at one time and place but in a series of piecemeal surrenders culminating on V-E (victory in Europe) Day, May 8, 1945.

The unplanned surrender had posed a touchy problem for the Big Three chiefs of state: British Prime Minister Winston Churchill, U.S. President Franklin D. Roosevelt, and Soviet Premier Josef Stalin. They agreed unanimously not only that surrender should be unconditional, but also that it should take place simultaneously on all fronts. Behind this second resolve was the Russian suspicion that Germany would succeed in making a separate peace with Great Britain and the United States and the western Allies' memory of Nazi-Soviet collaboration from August 1939 to June 1941. Even with seeming agreement among the Allies, the road to unconditional surrender proved to be as bumpy as it was long. The major sign posts along the road were the following:

July 25, 1943. The first break in the Axis alliance comes when Benito Mussolini resigns as Italian premier and is replaced by Marshal Pietro Badoglio.

September 8, 1943. Badoglio surrenders Italy on the eve of the Allied landing at Salerno, but Nazi troops install Mussolini as puppet head of German-occupied Italy, September 12.

February 1945. At Yalta, U.S.S.R., the Big Three chiefs of government issue a joint statement: "It is our inflexible purpose to destroy German militarism and nazism and to ensure that Germany will never again be able to disturb the peace of the world.... It is not our purpose to destroy the people of Germany, but only when nazism and militarism have been extirpated will there be hope for a decent life for the Germans and a place for them in the comity of nations."

April 23, 1945. U.S. troops cross the Po River and resistance on the Italian front collapses.

April 25, 1945. U.S. and Soviet troops meet at Torgau in the heart of Germany.

April 29, 1945. All German forces on the Italian front surrender, to be effective May 2.

April 30, 1945. The suicide of Adolph Hitler gives German leadership to Grand Adm. Karl Doenitz.

May 1, 1945. On Lueneberg Heath, German troops in Belgium, the Netherlands, and northern Germany surrender.

May 7, 1945. In Reims, the unconditional surrender of all German military forces is signed, to become effective at 11:01 p.m. the following day.

May 8, 1945. V-E Day. At Soviet insistence, formal instruments of unconditional surrender are signed in Berlin.

May 23, 1945. The principal members of the German government are arrested for alleged war crimes.

June 5, 1945. The Declaration on Germany is issued. By this instrument, the four Allied nations (now including France) assume complete political control of Germany.

Americans view bomb damage to the Reichstag buildings in Berlin. (239-RC-16-17, National Archives)

The Surrender in the Southwest

The Allied drive across the Po River in northern Italy led to the first installment of Germany's piecemeal surrender. There were many delays and false starts. The German negotiators had to hide their efforts from Hitler—and often from each other. Finally, representatives for both sides reached an agreement on terms and convened at Caserta, Italy, to sign the surrender document.

At the simple ceremony on April 29, 1945, a member of Col. Gen. Heinrich von Vietinghoff-Scheel's staff yielded up all the armed services in the German Southwest Command. A second German signature was that of SS Gen. Karl Wolff, whose organization had assumed a major role in the Nazi occupation of northern Italy after the Badoglio surrender in 1943. The acceptance was signed on behalf of Field Marshal Sir Harold Alexander, Supreme Allied Commander in the Mediterranean Theater.

Even though this was to be only a local surrender, the Allied commanders were enjoined to secure Soviet assent lest Stalin feel justified in his earlier accusation that Truman and Churchill were scheming at a separate peace. Although Stalin finally gave his approval and Soviet Maj. Gen. Alexi Kislenko attended the signing, the circumstances of the surrender in Italy magnified the always-present Russian suspicions. This was a factor in the later Soviet insistence on a second surrender at Berin, superseding the Reims surrender.

The Surrender in the Northwest

Like so many other events in military history, the signing of the *Instrument of Surrender of All German Armed Forces in Holland, in Northwest Germany Including All Islands, and in Denmark* took place on May 4, 1945, in a tent, on this occasion at the headquarters of British Field Marshal Sir Bernard Law Montgomery on Lueneberg Heath in the German state of lower Saxony. While regarded as a tactical surrender of forces in the field only, the Lueneburg Heath document, in article 5, states this surrender to be "superseded by any general instrument of surrender imposed by or on behalf of the Allied Powers," thus anticipating the unconditional surrender of the German nation at a later date.

The signers for Germany were, in order of seniority, Gen. Adm. Hans Georg von Friedeburg, chief German negotiator and commander in chief of the German Navy; Lt. Gen. Eberhard Kinzel, chief of staff to Field Marshal Ernst Busch, commander in chief of the German armies in the Northwest; Rear Adm. Gerhard Wagner, director of the German Military Cabinet; and staff officers Col. Fritz Poleck and Maj. Hans Jochen Friedal. Field Marshal Montgomery, commander of the British-Canadian 21st Army Group, signed the document with the authorization and as the representative of the Supreme Commander, Allied Expeditionary Force, General of the Army Dwight D. Eisenhower. (Montgomery also made a handwritten addition to the first article to include naval ships in this surrender.)

Preparing for a General Surrender

On May 6, Grand Adm. Karl Doenitz, who had become head of the Third Reich on Hitler's death, authorized Col. Gen. Alfred Jodl to conclude a general German surrender with General Eisenhower. The text of this order reads "I authorize Colonel General Jodl, Chief of the Operations' Staff in the High Command of the Armed Forces, to conclude an armistice agreement with the headquarters of General Eisenhower."

The new German approach met the demands of Supreme Headquarters, Allied Expeditionary Force (SHAEF), for a total, unconditional surrender of all German forces on both the western and eastern fronts. Doenitz and other German leaders had hoped until the last minute to make a separate peace with the British and American armies while continuing to resist the Soviet advance in the East or at least making some arrangement whereby German troops could avoid surrending to Soviet armies. These alternatives, clearly contrary to the spirit and letter of accords reached at summit conferences between the Big Three heads of government, were rejected out of hand by General Eisenhower, at whose insistence the first instruments of unconditional surrender were signed the following morning in Reims.

U.S. soldier takes refuge in a doorway during a hunt for German snipers in Cologne, March 1945. (208-AA-34P-2, National Archives)

The Surrender of all German Forces

The unconditional surrender of the German Third Reich was signed in the early morning hours of Monday, May 7, 1945; the time on the documents is noted as 0241 hours, or 2:41 a.m. The scene was the war room at SHAEF, located in the Professional and Technical School at Reims, a historic city in Northeastern France that had been almost completely leveled by the Germans during the war.

Across the conference table, representatives of the four Allied Powers—France, Great Britain, the Soviet Union, and the United States—faced the three German officers delegated by President Doenitz: Col. Gen. Alfred Jodl, who alone had been authorized to sign the surrender document; Gen. Adm. Hans Georg von Friedeburg, a chief negotiator here as on Lueneberg Heath; and Maj. Friedrich Wilhelm Oxenius, an aide to Jodl.

Lt. Gen. Walter Bedell Smith, SHAEF chief of staff, led the Allied delegation as the representative of General Eisenhower, who had refused to meet with the Germans until the surrender had been accomplished. Other American officers present were Maj. Gen. Harold R. Bull and Gen. Carl Spaatz.

British observers were Adm. Sir Harold Burrough, Lt. Gen. Sir Fred Morgan (SHAEF deputy chief of staff), and Air Marshal J. M. Robb. Maj. Gen. Ivan Sousloparov, head of the Soviet mission to France, represented the Soviet High Command; he was accompanied by Lt. Ivan Chermiaev and Senior Lt. Col. Ivan Zenkovitch as interpreters. Representing the French chief of staff (Gen. Alphonse Pierre Juin) was Maj. Gen. Francois Sevez.

The surrender document signed at Reims at 0241 hours on May 7, 1945, was not the official document that had been authorized in July 1944 by Churchill, Roosevelt, and Stalin. The July 1944 instrument had been produced through the arduous labors of the European Advisory Commission (EAC), which was set up in 1943 to work out the details of the unconditional German surrender and to propose specific solutions to the political and economic problems that were anticipated in postwar Germany.

The 45th Division in Nuernberg's Luitpole Arena after the capture of the city on April 20, 1945. (208-AA-33TT-7, National Archives)

Churchill, Roosevelt, and Stalin meet at the Livadia Palace at Yalta in February 1945. (FDR Library)

Although the EAC surrender document had been sent to General Eisenhower, two intervening developments deterred SHAEF officials from using it at Reims. First, France had been added as a signatory, causing the 1944 draft to be regarded by SHAEF as preliminary only. Second, the Big Three, meeting at Yalta in February 1945, had decided to add the word "dismemberment" to the calls for disarmament and demobilization already included in their guidelines for Germany's future, expressing thereby a determination to prevent further German militarism by partitioning the country into separate political units. The EAC drew up a new surrender document incorporating these changes.

SHAEF officials concluded, however, that political and other considerations should be settled at a high civilian level after the cessation of hostilities. Accordingly, they drew up their own military document, one directed only at ending the fighting and halting further bloodshed. Article 4 of the *Act of Military Surrender,* however, like Article 5 of the Lueneberg Heath *Instrument of Surrender,* looks ahead to additional accords. Inserted at the urgent behest of John Winant, U.S. Ambassador to Great Britain and representative to EAC, it ensured that the purely military surrenders of May 7 and 8 would be supplemented later by a general political surrender that contained the EAC provisions.

The more than 44 hours between the signing of the *Act of Military Surrender* and the cease-fire to take place at 2301 hours, or 11:01 p.m., on May 8 represented a concession to the Germans by SHAEF, one that unintentionally allowed more German troops to be moved westward for surrender to American or British and Commonwealth forces rather than to those of the Soviet Union.

Signers of the surrender document were Col. Gen. Alfred Jodl, on behalf of the German High Command; Lt. Gen. Walter Bedell Smith, representing General Eisenhower; Maj. Gen. Ivan Sousloparov, fulfilling the Big Three agreement that a Soviet representative would take part in any ceremony of total surrender; and Maj. Gen. Francois Sevez, signing as a witness for France.

Relaying the Surrender Orders

A second document signed at Reims contains orders from General Smith about procedures for disseminating detailed surrender instructions to German army and air force units on the western front. The specific orders were to come from the Allied unit commanders to their German counterparts.

The Surrender of German Naval Forces

The longest by far of the Reims documents contains a series of instructions for the surrender of all German naval forces, both surface and undersea. It was signed by Adm. Sir Harold Burrough on behalf of General Eisenhower. Both this document and the one previously mentioned (relating to army and air forces) emphasize the concern of SHAEF officials at Reims with bringing military activities to a halt and leaving the broader and more general provisions of surrender to a later time.

agreement. As a consequence, a critical phrase in the document is "with plenary powers," powers not delegated to Sousloparov. Thus a meeting was scheduled the following day in Berlin in response to Soviet concern that the Reims ceremony had given the impression of being the separate German surrender to the American and British forces that Doenitz had sought.

Third U.S. Army troops cross to the east bank of the Rhine, March 23, 1945. (208-AA-37T-6, National Archives)

Agreement for Formal Ratification

An agreement to meet at a later date—to be specified by General Eisenhower in his capacity as Supreme Commander, Allied Expeditionary Force—for a formal ratification of the unconditional surrender was also signed by Colonel General Jodl at the Reims ceremony.

Major General Sousloparov had been sent to Reims by the Soviet High Command to take part in the negotiations, but he was not empowered to sign any

Authorization to Execute Ratification

With a letter, Grand Adm. Karl Doenitz, now also the German president, authorized the signing of the formal unconditional surrender of Germany. Following the specifications of the final Reims document signed by General Jodl, Doenitz appointed three men to represent the German nation in the ceremony at Berlin on May 8: General Field Marshal Wilhelm Keitel; General Admiral Hans Georg von Friedeburg, a participant at both the Lueneberg Heath and Reims ceremonies; and Col. Gen. Hans Juergen Stumpf.

The letter reads: "I authorize General Field Marshal Keitel as chief of the High Command of the Armed Forces and simultaneously as Commander in Chief of the Army, General Admiral von Friedeburg as Commander in Chief of the Navy, Colonel General Stumpf as representative of the Commander in Chief of the Air Force to ratify the unconditional capitulation of the German fighting forces to the Commander in Chief of the Allied Expeditionary Forces and the Soviet High Command."

The Instrument of Surrender

To reassure the Soviet Union that the western Allies had no intention of concluding a separate peace with Germany, General Eisenhower requested that the Soviet representative in his theater, Major General Sousloparov, be authorized to participate in the Reims negotiations. But after the signing of the Reims accord, Soviet chief of staff General Alexei Antonov notified SHAEF that German troops continued to fight against Soviet forces, while scarcely resisting in the West. Thus the Reims surrender continued to resemble a separate truce on the western front, thereby belying Allied unity. The Soviet command wanted the Act of Military Surrender, with certain additions and alterations, to be signed at Berlin.

To the Soviets, the documents signed at Berlin on May 8, 1945, represented the official, legal surrender of the Third Reich. The U.S., British, and French governments regarded it as a symbol of Allied unity, east and west, and as merely the more formal of the two ceremonies ending the war.

Unlike the Reims documents, which were authoritative only in their English text, the surrender documents signed at Berlin on May 8, 1945, were written and signed separately in the English, Russian, and German languages.

General Dwight D. Eisenhower had originally planned to attend the ceremony at Berlin in his capacity as Supreme Commander, Allied Expeditionary Force. But because the Soviet plenary representative was to be Marshal Georgi Zhukov, a group commander well below him in rank, Eisenhower selected SHAEF deputy supreme commander, British Air Marshal Sir Arthur

Tedder. Protocol specified that Tedder sign as Eisenhower's representative and Zhukov on behalf of the Red Army. General Jean de Lattre de Tassigny and General Carl Spaatz signed as witnesses. Signing for Germany were Keitel, Von Friedeburg, and Stumpf, as designated by Doenitz.

The Berlin document had few significant changes from the one signed a day earlier at Reims. The phrase "Supreme High Command of the Red Army" was substituted for "Soviet High Command"; article 2 was altered to require that Germany "disarm completely"; and the demand that ships and military equipment not be damaged was made more detailed.

President Truman's V-E Day Proclamation

As part of the V-E Day celebration, President Harry Truman issued a proclamation designating the following Sunday, May 13, as a day of prayer and thanksgiving. In this proclamation the Presidnet notes the "final and unconditional surrender" of Germany but warns that victory must still be won "in the East" (Japan). Only then will the world be "cleansed of the evil." This victory would come in a little over 3 months with the surrender of the Japanese government, August 14 (U.S. time).

A Red Army soldier lifts a Nazi flag out of the debris in Berlin. (242-GAV-178a, National Archives)

Surveying bomb damage to Frankfurt, Germany. (RG 243, IIIa (970)6, National Archives)

Epilogue

As a means of bringing about an orderly transition of power in Germany, the Allies allowed the government of Grand Admiral Karl Doenitz to remain in power for 16 days. On May 23, 1945, however, the principal members of the government were taken into custody for trial as war criminals.

On June 5, the Allied commander in chief issued the Declaration on Germany, which represented the official assumption of political control of the nation by the four occupying powers—the United States, the Soviet Union, Great Britain, and France. This instrument was to replace the broader political surrender that had been anticipated in the Reims and Berlin surrender documents.

Of the Germans who were involved in the surrender ceremonies in Reims and Berlin, Doenitz received a 100-year prison sentence and Keitel and Jodl were hanged after trial at Nurenburg; Von Friedeburg committed suicide before his trial.

For Further Reading:

Ambrose, Stephen E. *The Supreme Commander: The War Years of General Dwight D. Eisenhower.* Garden City, NY: Doubleday, 1970.

Donitz, Karl. *Memoirs: Ten Years and Twenty Days.* Translated by R.H. Stevens. Cleveland, OH: World, 1959.

Eisenhower, David. *Eisenhower at War, 1943-1945.* New York: Random House, 1986.

Eisenhower, Dwight D. *Crusade in Europe.* Garden City, NY: Doubleday, 1948.

Kecskemeti, Paul. *Strategic Surrender: The Politics of Victory and Defeat.* Stanford, CA: Stanford University Press, 1958.

Murphy, Robert D. *Diplomat Among Warriors.* Garden City, NY: Doubleday, 1964.

Steinert, Marlis G. *Twenty-three Days: The Final Collapse of Nazi Germany.* Translated by Richard Barry. New York: Walker, 1969.

Zhukov, Georgii K. *The Memoirs of Marshal Zhukov.* Translated by Theodore Shabad. New York: Delacorte, 1971.

THE FACSIMILES

INSTRUMENT OF LOCAL SURRENDER OF GERMAN AND
OTHER FORCES UNDER THE COMMAND OR CONTROL
OF THE GERMAN COMMANDER-IN-CHIEF SOUTHWEST

---

1. The German Commander-in-Chief Southwest hereby surrenders unconditionally all the forces under his command or control on land, at sea and in the air and places himself and these forces unconditionally at the disposal of the Supreme Allied Commander, Mediterranean Theatre of Operations.

2. All armed forces under the command or control of the German Commander-in-Chief Southwest will cease all hostilities on land, at sea and in the air at 1200 hours (Greenwich mean time) on 2 May 1945. The German Commander-in-Chief Southwest undertakes to arrange accordingly.

3. The German Commander-in-Chief Southwest undertakes to carry out the orders set out in Appendices A, B and C and any further orders of the Supreme Allied Commander, Mediterranean Theatre of Operations. Disobedience of such orders or failure to comply with them will be dealt with in accordance with the accepted laws and usages of war.

4. This instrument will enter into force immediately on signature, and the orders in Appendices A, B and C will become effective on the date and at the time specified in paragraph 2 above.

5. This instrument and accompanying orders are drawn up in the English and German languages. The English version is the authentic text. If any doubt as to meaning or interpretation arises, the decision of the Supreme Allied Commander is final.

SECRET

"Secret" instrument of local surrender—Italy

6. This instrument is independent of, without prejudice to, and shall be superseded by any general instrument of surrender imposed by or on behalf of the United Nations and applicable to GERMANY and the German armed forces as a whole.

VICTOR VON SCHWEINITZ,
Lieutenant Colonel in
  the General Staff of
  Army Group C,
for Colonel General VON
  VIETINGHOFF-SCHEEL,
Commander-in-Chief South-
  west and Commander-in-
  Chief of Army Group C.

W. D. MORGAN,
Lieutenant General,
Chief of Staff,
for Field Marshal The
  Honourable Sir Harold
  R.L.G. ALEXANDER,
Supreme Allied Commander
  of the Mediterranean
  Theatre of Operations

EUGEN WENNER,
SS-Sturmbannführer and
  Major in the Waffen-SS,
for SS-Obergruppenführer
  and General of the Waffen-
  SS WOLFF,
Supreme Commander of SS and
  Police and plenipotentiary
  General of the German Wehr-
  macht in Italy.

Signed at CASERTA, Italy.

29th April 1945

      400 .... hours

<u>Instrument of Surrender</u>

of

<u>All</u> German armed forces in HOLLAND, in

northwest Germany including all islands,

and in DENMARK.

1. The German Command agrees to the surrender of all German armed
   forces in HOLLAND, in northwest GERMANY including the FRISIAN
   ISLANDS and HELIGOLAND and all other islands, in SCHLESWIG-
   HOLSTEIN, and in DENMARK, to the C.-in-C. 21 Army Group.
   This to include all naval ships in these areas.
   These forces to lay down their arms and to surrender unconditionally.

2. All hostilities on land, on sea, or in the air by German forces
   in the above areas to cease at 0800 hrs. British Double Summer Time
   on Saturday 5 May 1945.

3. The German command to carry out at once, and without argument or
   comment, all further orders that will be issued by the Allied
   Powers on any subject.

4. Disobedience of orders, or failure to comply with them, will be
   regarded as a breach of these surrender terms and will be dealt
   with by the Allied Powers in accordance with the accepted laws
   and usages of war.

5. This instrument of surrender is independent of, without prejudice
   to, and will be superseded by any general instrument of surrender
   imposed by or on behalf of the Allied Powers and applicable to Germany
   and the German armed forces as a whole.

6. This instrument of surrender is written in English and in German.

   The English version is the authentic text.

7. The decision of the Allied Powers will be final if any doubt or
   dispute arises as to the meaning or interpretation of the surrender
   terms.

v. Friedeburg.

Kinzel.

R. Wagner.

[signature]

[signature]

B. L. Montgomery
Field-Marshal

4 May 1945
1830 hrs.

Instrument of surrender—Holland

C056076

Hauptquartier, den 6. Mai 1945.

Ich bevollmächtige Generaloberst J o d l ,
Chef des Wehrmachtführungsstabes im Oberkommando
der Wehrmacht, zum Abschluss eines Waffenstill-
standsabkommens mit dem Hauptquartier des Generals
E i s e n h o w e r .

Dönitz

Großadmiral.

WR 5-16-45

Doenitz's authorization to Jodl

Only this text in English is authoritative

ACT OF MILITARY SURRENDER

1.   We the undersigned, acting by authority of the German High Command, hereby surrender unconditionally to the Supreme Commander, Allied Expeditionary Force and simultaneously to the Soviet High Command all forces on land, sea, and in the air who are at this date under German control.

2.   The German High Command will at once issue orders to all German military, naval and air authorities and to all forces under German control to cease active operations at 2301 hours Central European time on 8 May   and to remain in the positions occupied at that time. No ship, vessel, or aircraft is to be scuttled, or any damage done to their hull, machinery or equipment.

3.   The German High Command will at once issue to the appropriate commanders, and ensure the carrying out of any further orders issued by the Supreme Commander, Allied Expeditionary Force and by the Soviet High Command.

4.   This act of military surrender is without prejudice to, and will be superseded by any general instrument of surrender imposed by, or on behalf of the United Nations and applicable to GERMANY and the German armed forces as a whole.

- 1 -

5.   In the event of the German High Command
or any of the forces under their control failing
to act in accordance with this Act of Surrender,
the Supreme Commander, Allied Expeditionary Force
and the Soviet High Command will take such punitive
or other action as they deem appropriate.

Signed at *Rheims* at 0241 on the   7th   day of May, 1945.
            France

On behalf of the German High Command.

[signature]

IN THE PRESENCE OF

On behalf of the Supreme Commander,   On behalf of the Soviet
    Allied Expeditionary Force.   High Command.

[signature]   *[signature]*

[signature] -2-

Major General, French Army
        (Witness)

SUPREME HEADQUARTERS
ALLIED EXPEDITIONARY FORCE

SERIAL 1

ORDERS BY THE SUPREME COMMANDER,

ALLIED EXPEDITIONARY FORCE RELATING TO

ARMY AND AIR FORCES UNDER GERMAN CONTROL

1.   Local commanders of Army and Air Forces
under German control on the Western Front, in
NORWAY and in the CHANNEL ISLANDS will hold themselves
in readiness to receive detailed orders for the
surrender of their forces from the Supreme Commander's
subordinate commanders opposite their front.

2.   In the case of NORWAY the Supreme
Commander's representatives will be the General
Officer Commanding-in-Chief, Scottish Command and
Air Officer Commanding 13 Group RAF.

3.   In the case of the CHANNEL ISLANDS the
Supreme Commander's representatives will be the
General Officer Commanding-in-Chief, Southern
Command and Air Officer Commanding 10 Group RAF.

Signed........................
For the Supreme Commander, AEF.

Dated 0241 7th May, 1945.

Rheims France

Orders related to surrender of German Army and Air forces

SPECIAL ORDERS BY THE SUPREME COMMANDER, ALLIED

EXPEDITIONARY FORCE TO THE GERMAN HIGH COMMAND

RELATING TO NAVAL FORCES

PART I GENERAL

Definition of Naval Forces

1.   For the purpose of these orders all formations,
units and personnel of the German Navy together with the
Marine Kusten Polizei shall be referred to as the German
Naval Forces.

2.   Members of the Marine Kusten Polizei will
immediately be placed under the command of the appropriate
German Naval Commanders who will be responsible for their
disarmament and discipline, as well as for their
maintenance and supply where applicable, to the same
extent and degree as for units of the German Navy.

German Naval Representatives and information required
immediately

3.   The German High Command will despatch within
48 hours after the surrender becomes effective, a res-
ponsible Flag Officer to the Allied Naval Commander,
Expeditionary Force at his Headquarters. This
Flag Officer will furnish the Allied Naval Commander,
Expeditionary Force, with:-

a.   Corrected copies of charts showing all
minefields in Western European waters, including the
BALTIC as far as LUBECK (inclusive) which have been laid
by German and German-controlled vessels or aircraft,
positions of all wrecks, booms and other underwater
obstructions in this area, details of the German convoy
routes and searched channels and of all buoys, lights
and other navigational aids in this area. The appropriate
navigational publications are also required.

-1-

Orders related to surrender of German naval forces

b. all Naval personnel ashore are to remain in their establishments.

17. The German High Command will be responsible for the immediate and total disarmament of all naval personnel on shore. The orders issued to the German High Command in respect of the disarmament and war material of land forces will apply also to naval personnel on shore.

Signed...................
For the Supreme Commander, AEF.

Dated 0241 7 th May 1945
Rheims, France

ANNEXURE 'A'

SURRENDER OF GERMAN 'U' BOAT FLEET

To all 'U' Boats at sea:

Carry out the following instructions forthwith which have been given by the Allied Representatives

(A) Surface immediately and remain surfaced.

(B) Report immediately in P/L your position in latitude and longitude and number of your 'U' Boat to nearest British, US, Canadian or Soviet coast W/T station on 500 kc/s (600 metres) and to call sign GZZ 10 on one of the following high frequencies: 16845 - 12685 or 5970 kc/s.

(C) Fly a large black or blue flag by day.

(D) Burn navigation lights by night.

(E) Jettison all ammunition, remove breachblocks from guns and render torpedoes safe by removing pistols. All mines are to be rendered safe.

(F) Make all signals in P/L.

(G) Follow strictly the instructions for proceeding to Allied ports from your present area given in immediately following message.

(H) Observe strictly the orders of Allied Representatives to refrain from scuttling or in any way damaging your 'U' Boat.

2. These instructions will be repeated at two-hour intervals until further notice.

U-boat Annex

UNDERTAKING

GIVEN BY CERTAIN GERMAN EMISSARIES

TO THE ALLIED HIGH COMMANDS

It is agreed by the German emissaries undersigned that the following German officers will arrive at a place and time designated by the Supreme Commander, Allied Expeditionary Force, and the Soviet High Command prepared, with plenary powers, to execute a formal ratification on behalf of the German High Command of this act of Unconditional Surrender of the German armed forces.

Chief of the High Command

Commander-in-Chief of the Army

Commander-in-Chief of the Navy

Commander-in-Chief of the Air Forces.

SIGNED

Jodl

Representing the German High Command.

DATED 0241 7th may 1945
Rheims, France

Agreement for formal ratification

A b s c h r i f t.

Der Oberste Befehlshaber
der Wehrmacht

Hauptquartier, den **7.5.45.**

_/Bitte in der Antwort vorstehendes
Geschäftszeichen, das Datum und
kurzen Inhalt anzugeben./_

ICH BEVOLLMÄCHTIGE

GENERALFELDMARSCHALL   K E I T E L

ALS   CHEF DES OBERKOMMANDOS DER

WEHRMACHT UND ZUGLEICH ALS OBER-

BEFEHLSHABER DES HEERES,

GENERALADMIRAL   VON   FRIEDEBURG

ALS OBERBEFEHLSHABER DER KRIEGSMARINE,

GENERALOBERST   S T U M P F

ALS VERTRETER DES OBERBEFEHLSHABERS

DER LUFTWAFFE

ZUR RATIFIZIERUNG DER BEDINGUNGSLOSEN

KAPITULATION DER DEUTSCHEN STREITKRÄFTE GEGEN-

ÜBER DEM OBERBEFEHLSHABER DER ALLIIERTEN

EXPEDITIONSSTREITKRÄFTE UND DEM SOWJET-OBER-

KOMMANDO.

DÖNITZ

GROSSADMIRAL.

Siegel.

Beglaubigt (Cornelius)

Authorization to execute ratification (in German)

ACT OF MILITARY SURRENDER

1.   We the undersigned, acting by authority
of the German High Command, hereby surrender
unconditionally to the Supreme Commander, Allied
Expeditionary Force and simultaneously to the
Supreme High Command of the Red Army all forces
on land, at sea, and in the air who are at this
date under German control.

2.   The German High Command will at once
issue orders to all German military, naval and
air authorities and to all forces under German
control to cease active operations at 2301 hours
Central European time on 8th May 1945, to remain
in the positions occupied at that time and to
disarm completely, handing over their weapons and
equipment to the local allied commanders or officers
designated by Representatives of the Allied Supreme
Commands.   No ship, vessel, or aircraft is to be
scuttled, or any damage done to their hull,
machinery or equipment, and also to machines of all
kinds, armament, apparatus, and all the technical
means of prosecution of war in general.

- 1 -

Instrument of surrender—Berlin (English)

3. The German High Command will at once issue to the appropriate commanders, and ensure the carrying out of any further orders issued by the Supreme Commander, Allied Expeditionary Force and by the Supreme High Command of the Red Army.

4. This act of military surrender is without prejudice to, and will be superseded by any general instrument of surrender imposed by, or on behalf of the United Nations and applicable to GERMANY and the German armed forces as a whole.

5. In the event of the German High Command or any of the forces under their control failing to act in accordance with this Act of Surrender, the Supreme Commander, Allied Expeditionary Force and the Supreme High Command of the Red Army will take such punitive or other action as they deem appropriate.

- 2 -

6. This Act is drawn up in the English,
Russian and German languages. The English and
Russian are the only authentic texts.

Signed at *Berlin* on the   8.   day of May, 1945

On behalf of the German High Command

- -

IN THE PRESENCE OF:

On behalf of the
Supreme Commander
Allied Expeditionary Force

On behalf of the
Supreme High Command of the
Red Army

At the signing also were present as witnesses:

General Commanding in Chief
First French Army

General, Commanding
United States Strategic Air Forces

-5-

АКТ О ВОЕННОЙ КАПИТУЛЯЦИИ.

1. Мы, нижеподписавшиеся, действуя от имени Германского Верховного Командования, соглашаемся на безоговорочную капитуляцию всех наших вооруженных сил на суше, на море и в воздухе, а также всех сил, находящихся в настоящее время под немецким командованием, - Верховному Главнокомандованию Красной Армии и одновременно Верховному Командованию Союзных Экспедиционных сил.

2. Германское Верховное командование немедленно издает приказы всем немецким командующим сухопутными, морскими и воздушными силами и всем силам, находящимся под германским командованием, прекратить военные действия в 23-01 час по Центрально-Европейскому времени 8 мая 1945 года, остаться на своих местах, где они находятся в это время, и полностью разоружиться, передав все их оружие и военное имущество местным союзным командующим или офицерам, выделенным представителями Союзных Верховных Командований, не разрушать и не причинять никаких повреждений пароходам, судам и самолетам, их двигателям, корпусам и оборудованию, а также машинам, вооружению, аппаратам и всем вообще военно-техническим средствам ведения войны.

2.-

3. Германское Верховное Командование немедленно выделит соответствующих командиров и обеспечит выполнение всех дальнейших приказов, изданных Верховным Главнокомандованием Красной Армии и Верховным Командованием Союзных Экспедиционных сил.

4. Этот акт не будет являться препятствием к замене его другим генеральным документом о капитуляции, заключенным Об'единенными Нациями или от их имени, применимым к Германии и германским вооруженным силам в целом.

5. В случае, если немецкое Верховное Командование или какие-либо вооруженные силы, находящиеся под его командованием, не будут действовать в соответствии с этим актом о капитуляции, Верховное Командование Красной Армии, а также Верховное Командование Союзных Экспедиционных сил, предпримут такие карательные меры, или другие действия, которые они сочтут необходимыми.

6. Этот акт составлен на английском, русском и немецком языках. Только английский и русский тексты являются аутентичными.

3.-

Подписано 8 мая 1945 года в гор. БЕРЛИНЕ.

От имени Германского Верховного Командования:

В присутствии:

По уполномочию Верховного
Командующего Экспедиционными
силами Союзников
ГЛАВНОГО МАРШАЛА АВИАЦИИ
ТЕДДЕРА

По уполномочию Верховного
Главнокомандования Красной
Армии
МАРШАЛА СОВЕТСКОГО СОЮЗА
Г.ЖУКОВА

При подписании также присутствовали в качестве
свидетелей:

Командующий Стратегическими
Воздушными силами США
ГЕНЕРАЛ
СПААТС

Главнокомандующий Французской
Армией
ГЕНЕРАЛ ДЕЛАТР
де ТАССИНЫ

KAPITULATIONSERKLAERUNG.

1. Wir, die hier Unterzeichneten, handelnd in Vollmacht
fuer und im Namen des Oberkommandos der Deutschen Wehrmacht,
erklaeren hiermit die bedingungslose Kapitulation aller am
gegenwaertigen Zeitpunkt unter deutschem Befehl stehenden
oder von Deutschland beherrschten Streitkraefte auf dem Lande,
auf der See und in der Luft gleichzeitig gegenueber dem
Obersten Befehlshaber der Alliierten Expeditions Streitkraefte
und dem Oberkommando der Roten Armee.

2. Das Oberkommando der Deutschen Wehrmacht wird
unverzueglich allen Behoerden der deutschen Land-,See- und
Luftstreitkraefte und allen von Deutschland beherrschten
Streitkraeften den Befehl geben, die Kampfhandlungen um 2301
Uhr Mitteleuropaeischer Zeit am 8 Mai einzustellen und in den
Stellungen zu verbleiben, die sie an diesem Zeitpunkt inne-
haben und sich vollstaendig zu entwaffnen, indem sie Waffen
und Geraete an die oertlichen Alliierten Befehlshaber
beziehungsweise an die von den Alliierten Vertretern zu
bestimmenden Offiziere abliefern. Kein Schiff, Boot oder
Flugzeug irgendeiner Art darf versenkt werden, noch duerfen
Schiffsruempfe, maschinelle Einrichtungen, Ausruestungsgegen-
staende, Maschinen irgendwelcher Art, Waffen, Apparaturen,
technische Gegenstaende, die Kriegszwecken im Allgemeinen
dienlich sein koennen, beschaedigt werden.

3. Das Oberkommando der Deutschen Wehrmacht wird
unverzueglich den zustaendigen Befehlshabern alle von dem
Obersten Befehlshaber der Alliierten Expeditions Streitkraefte
und dem Oberkommando der Roten Armee erlassenen zusaetzlichen
Befehle weitergeben und deren Durchfuehrung sicherstellen.

4. Diese Kapitulationserklaerung ist ohne Praejudiz fuer
irgendwelche an ihre Stelle tretenden allgemeinen Kapitulations-
bestimmungen, die durch die Vereinten Nationen und in deren
Namen Deutschland und der Deutschen Wehrmacht auferlegt werden
moegen.

5. Falls das Oberkommando der Deutschen Wehrmacht oder
irgendwelche ihm unterstehende oder von ihm beherrschte
Streitkraefte es versaeumen sollten, sich gemaess den
Bestimmungen dieser Kapitulations-Erklaerung zu verhalten,

Instrument of surrender—Berlin (German)

C056107

werden der Oberste Befehlshaber der Alliierten Expeditions Streitkraefte und das Oberkommando der Roten Armee alle diejenigen Straf- und anderen Massnahmen ergreifen, die sie als zweckmaessig erachten.

6. Diese Erklaerung ist in englischer, russischer und deutscher Sprache abgefasst. Allein massgebend sind die englische und die russische Fassung.

Unterzeichnet zu *Berlin* am *8.* Mai 1945

[signatures]

Fuer das Oberkommando der Deutschen Wehrmacht.

In Gegenwart von:

[signature]

Fuer den Obersten Befehlshaber der Alliierten Expeditions- Streitkraefte.

Fuer das Oberkommando der Roten Armee

[signature]

Bei der Unterzeichnung waren als Zeugen auch zugegen:

[signature]

General, Oberstkommandierender der Ersten Franzoesischen Armee

[signature]

Kommandierender General der Strategischen Luftstreitkraefte der Vereinigten Staaten

BY THE PRESIDENT OF THE UNITED STATES OF AMERICA

A PROCLAMATION

The Allied armies, through sacrifice and devotion and with God's help, have wrung from Germany a final and unconditional surrender. The western world has been freed of the evil forces which for five years and longer have imprisoned the bodies and broken the lives of millions upon millions of free-born men. They have violated their churches, destroyed their homes, corrupted their children, and murdered their loved ones. Our Armies of Liberation have restored freedom to these suffering peoples, whose spirit and will the oppressors could never enslave.

Much remains to be done. The victory won in the West must now be won in the East. The whole world must be cleansed of the evil from which half the world has been freed. United, the peace-loving nations have demonstrated in the West that their arms are stronger by far than the might of dictators or the tyranny of military cliques that once called us soft and weak. The power of our peoples to defend themselves against all enemies will be proved in the Pacific war as it has been proved in Europe.

For the triumph of spirit and of arms which we have won, and for its promise to peoples everywhere who join us in the love of freedom, it is fitting that we, as a nation, give thanks to Almighty God, who has strengthened us and given us the victory.

NOW, THEREFORE, I, HARRY S. TRUMAN, President of the United States of America, do hereby appoint Sunday, May 13, 1945, to be a day of prayer.

I call upon the people of the United States, whatever their faith, to unite in offering joyful thanks to God for the victory we

Page forty

Truman's V-E Day Proclamation

have won and to pray that He will support us to the end of our present struggle and guide us into the way of peace.

I also call upon my countrymen to dedicate this day of prayer to the memory of those who have given their lives to make possible our victory.

IN WITNESS WHEREOF, I have hereunto set my hand and caused the seal of the United States of America to be affixed.

Done at the City of Washington this eighth day of May in the year of our Lord nineteen hundred and forty-five and of the Independence of the United States of America the one hundred and sixty-ninth.

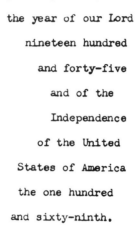

Harry Truman

By the President:

Joseph C. Grew

Acting Secretary of State.

3 08 PM

REGISTER